MADE FOR A MIRACLE
LEADER GUIDE

D1599345

Made for a Miracle
From Your Ordinary to God's *Extraordinary*

Book
978-1-5018-4138-5
978-1-5018-4139-2 eBook
978-1-5018-4140-8 Large Print

DVD
978-1-5018-4143-9

Leader Guide
978-1-5018-4141-5
978-1-5018-4142-1 eBook

Youth Study Book
978-1-5018-4150-7
978-1-5018-4151-4 eBook

Also by Mike Slaughter

Change the World
Christmas Is Not Your Birthday
Dare to Dream
Down to Earth
Hijacked
Momentum for Life
Money Matters
Real Followers
Renegade Gospel
shiny gods
Spiritual Entrepreneurs
The Christian Wallet
The Passionate Church
UnLearning Church
Upside Living in a Downside Economy

For more information, visit www.MikeSlaughter.com.

MIKE SLAUGHTER

MADE FOR A
MIRACLE

From Your Ordinary
to God's *Extraordinary*

Leader Guide
by Martha Bettis Gee

Abingdon Press / Nashville

MADE FOR A MIRACLE
FROM YOUR ORDINARY TO GOD'S EXTRAORDINARY
LEADER GUIDE

This book is printed on elemental chlorine-free paper.

ISBN 978-1-5018-4141-5

17 18 19 20 21 22 23 24 25 26 — 10 9 8 7 6 5 4 3 2 1

MANUFACTURED IN THE UNITED STATES OF AMERICA

Contents

To the Leader 7

1. You Were Made for a Miracle 12

2. Miracles Come with a Cost 20

3. The Miracle of Love. 29

4. Activate the Power of Faith 38

5. Activate the Power of Prayer 46

6. Activate Health and Healing 54

TO THE LEADER

Welcome! In this study, you have the opportunity to help a group of learners explore the possibility for miracles in all of our lives. The study is based on Mike Slaughter's book, *Made for a Miracle: From Your Ordinary to God's* Extraordinary.

Mike Slaughter is pastor emeritus and global ambassador for Ginghamsburg Church, a United Methodist congregation in Tipp City, Ohio, with four campuses that total over four thousand worshipers every Sunday. Slaughter believes that each of us was made for a miracle, but he emphasizes that the miracles are not passive. Miracles come at a cost and require something of us. In fact, when God acts, God always acts through people. As participants in the study will discover, God's miracles typically have two dimensions: divine intervention and human responsibility.

The author guides us as we discover that God releases miracles through us for God's purposes in our lives and the lives of others. Slaughter poses the question: Where is God calling you to heal, teach, preach, redeem, and restore that which is broken, struggling, or suffering in the world God loves?

The book and study are perfect for use during Lent, but they are designed to be used any time of year, in any church season.

Scripture tells us that where two or three are gathered together, we can be assured of the presence of the Holy Spirit, working in and through all those gathered. As you prepare to lead, pray for that presence and expect that you will experience it.

The study includes six sessions, and it makes use of the following components:

- The book *Made for a Miracle: From Your Ordinary to God's Extraordinary*;
- the DVD that accompanies the study;
- this Leader Guide.

Participants in the study will also need Bibles, as well as either a spiral-bound notebook for a journal or an electronic means of journaling, such as a tablet. If possible, notify those interested in the study in advance of the first session. Make arrangements for them to get copies of the book so they can read the introduction and chapter 1 before the first group meeting.

USING THIS GUIDE WITH YOUR GROUP

Because no two groups are alike, this guide has been designed to give you flexibility and choice in tailoring the sessions for your group. The session format is listed below. You may choose any or all of the activities, adapting them as you wish to meet the schedule and needs of your particular group.

The leader guide offers a basic session plan designed to be completed in a session of about 45 minutes in length. Select ahead of time which activities the group will do, for how long, and in what order. Depending on which activities you select, there may be special preparation needed. The leader is alerted in the session plan when advance preparation is needed.

Session Format

Planning the Session
    Session Goals
    Scriptural Foundation
    Special Preparation

Getting Started
    Opening Activity
    Opening Prayer

Learning Together
    Video Study and Discussion
    Book and Bible Study and Discussion

Wrapping Up
    Closing Activity
    Closing Prayer

HELPFUL HINTS

Preparing for the Session

- Pray for the leading of the Holy Spirit as you prepare for the study. Pray for discernment for yourself and for each member of the study group.
- Before each session, familiarize yourself with the content. Read the book chapter again.
- Depending on the length of time you have available for group meetings, you may or may not have time to do all the activities. Select the activities in advance that will work for your group time and interests.
- Choose the session elements you will use during the group session, including the specific discussion questions you plan to cover. Be prepared, however, to adjust the session as group members interact and as questions arise. Prepare

carefully, but allow space for the Holy Spirit to move in and through the group members and through you as facilitator.

- Prepare the room where the group will meet so that the space will enhance the learning process. Ideally, group members should be seated around a table or in a circle so that all can see each other. Movable chairs are best because the group will often be forming pairs or small groups for discussion.

- Bring a supply of Bibles for those who forget to bring their own. Also bring writing paper and pens for those participants who do not bring a journal or a tablet or other electronic means of journaling.

- For most sessions you will also need a chalkboard and chalk, a whiteboard and markers, or an easel with large sheets of paper and markers.

Shaping the Learning Environment

- Begin and end on time.
- Create a climate of openness, encouraging group members to participate as they feel comfortable.
- Remember that some people will jump right in with answers and comments, while others need time to process what is being discussed.
- If you notice that some group members seem never to be able to enter the conversation, ask them if they have thoughts to share. Give everyone a chance to talk, but keep the conversation moving. Moderate to prevent a few individuals from doing all the talking.
- Communicate the importance of group discussions and group exercises.
- If no one answers at first during discussions, do not be afraid of silence. Count silently to ten, then say something such as, "Would anyone like to go first?" If no one responds, venture an answer yourself and ask for comments.

- Model openness as you share with the group. Group members will follow your example. If you limit your sharing to a surface level, others will follow suit.
- Encourage multiple answers or responses before moving on.
- To help continue a discussion and give it greater depth, ask, "Why?" or "Why do you believe that?" or "Can you say more about that?"
- Affirm others' responses with comments such as "Great" or "Thanks" or "Good insight," especially if it's the first time someone has spoken during the group session.
- Monitor your own contributions. If you are doing most of the talking, back off so that you do not train the group to listen rather than speak up.
- Remember that you do not have all the answers. Your job is to keep the discussion going and encourage participation.

Managing the Session

- Honor the time schedule. If a session is running longer than expected, get consensus from the group before continuing beyond the agreed-upon ending time.
- Involve group members in various aspects of the group session, such as saying prayers or reading Scripture.
- Note that the session guides sometimes call for breaking into smaller groups or pairs. This gives everyone a chance to speak and participate fully. Mix up the groups; don't let the same people pair up for every activity.
- As always in discussions that may involve personal sharing, confidentiality is essential. Group members should never pass along stories that have been shared in the group. Remind the group members at each session: confidentiality is crucial to the success of this study.

1

You Were Made for a Miracle

Planning the Session

Session Goals

As a result of conversations and activities connected with this session, group members should begin to:

- explore what it means to continue to answer the call of Jesus;
- encounter how they might experience the truly miraculous as they journey with Jesus in the way of the cross;
- examine how they might discover their true identity and life purpose in Christ; and
- ponder how saying yes to God's will could empower them to become a healing source of God's miracles in people's lives.

Scriptural Foundation

When Jesus had called the Twelve together, he gave
them power and authority to drive out all demons and
to cure diseases, and he sent them out to proclaim the
kingdom of God and to heal the sick.

(Luke 9:1-2)

Special Preparation

- Have available a notebook or paper and pen or pencil for anyone who did not bring a notebook or an electronic device for journaling.
- On a large sheet of paper or a board, print the following questions for the opening activity.
  - o Who are you, Lord?
  - o Who is this about whom I hear such things?
  - o What shall I do with this Jesus who is called the Messiah?
- On another large sheet of paper or a different place on a board, print the following reflection questions from the end of the chapter for the reflecting activity:
  - o Where are you sensing God at work right now in your church or community through divine intervention intersecting with human initiative? How might you become a part of the miracle?
  - o Have you been praying for a miracle? What opportunities might you have to add your human initiative or resources toward God's divine intervention in your family, neighborhood, or workplace?
- For the closing activity, you will need index cards and pens or pencils for participants.

GETTING STARTED

Opening Activity

As participants arrive, welcome them to the study. Gather together. If participants are not familiar with one another, provide nametags and make introductions.

Refer group members to the first sentence in book chapter 1, which is the following question:

- Can you remember when the call to follow Jesus became personal?

Note that the author, Mike Slaughter, relates several ways in which Jesus' call may come to individuals. Ask each person to reflect in silence for a few moments on the following:

- When you first began to sense Jesus' call to you, how did he speak to you?

Form pairs, and ask participants to discuss this question with their partner. After allowing a few moments for discussion, invite volunteers to respond to the following:

- How does Jesus "speak" with you now?

Call attention to the posted reflection questions, what the author suggests are some of the most important questions we will ask in our lifetimes.

- Where are you sensing God at work right now in your church or community through divine intervention intersecting with human initiative? How might you become a part of the miracle?
- Have you been praying for a miracle? What opportunities might you have to add your human initiative or resources toward God's divine intervention in your family, neighborhood, or workplace?

Tell the group that in this study participants will explore how they might continue to answer these questions as they seek to encounter ways to follow Jesus more completely.

Opening Prayer

Pray together, using the following prayer or one of your own choosing:

Gracious God, guide our exploration as we try to discern more fully, and act more boldly, in answering Jesus' call to follow him. Make us more aware of your presence with us as together we encounter you in your word and in the collective insights of our time together. Amen.

LEARNING TOGETHER

Video Study and Discussion

In this study, participants will explore how God releases miracles through people, seeking to discern where God is calling them to heal and restore that which is broken, struggling, or suffering in the world God loves.

In session 1, viewers are introduced to Ron Will, who answered God's call to make real a vision for a recovery ministry. In turn, viewers will explore how they too might discover their true identity and life purpose in Christ.

- Ron Will notes that to be a part of God's miraculous work, you must both make yourself available and also be willing to go where God wants you to go. How did Ron make himself available?
- Ron's description of how Joshua Recovery Ministries came to be makes it clear that it was not just the result of one person's vision. What role did other members of the community of faith play?

15

- Ron notes that to take on a mission such as his, you had better have both passion and a call from God. Passion alone, he notes, is not enough to help you make it through the hard times. How do you respond to that?
- What do you think is the necessary role of passion in undertaking a mission calling? What else is needed beyond passion?

Book and Bible Study and Discussion

Explore Our Identity in Christ

If they have not already had a chance to do so, ask participants to quickly read over the information in chapter 1 under the heading "The Miracle of Transformation." Point out that the author poses the following question:

- Have you noticed that it was the nonreligious, ordinary, socially unacceptable, and religiously incorrect types whom Jesus chose to lead his movement?

Ask the group to name some of Jesus' first followers who fit this description. Discuss some of the following:

- What action did Jesus take with his own disciples to indicate they had a new identity?
- The author cites the story of Jacob from centuries before Jesus came on the scene. After an all-night wrestling match with God, God gave Jacob a new name. What was the meaning of Jacob's old name? What was the meaning of the new name that indicated his new identity?
- From that time forward, what mark or sign did Jacob carry in his body, and what does the author suggest was its significance? Is there something about you that serves as a reminder of your commitment to a sacrificial life of following Jesus?

16

- The author observes that the suffering and brokenness that are the result of sin cause us to lose our identity as children of God. He notes that we are reminded of our true identity in our baptisms. What does he suggest we boldly proclaim when the voices of darkness seek to make us question our identity?

Examine How One Partners in the Miraculous

Invite a volunteer to read aloud Luke 9:1-6, the passage in which is found this session's foundational Scripture. Then ask someone else to read aloud Luke 10:1-12, 17. Discuss some of the following:

- The author suggests that every miracle has two components that must act in tandem. What are they?
- He notes that each of us brings our unique set of spiritual gifts, talents, and resources to function together as Christ's body to carry out Jesus' mission in the world—and this is what it means to be church. How do you respond? Would you concur with this definition of church? If not, how would you define church? What would you add or subtract?
- What do you think it means that as Jesus' disciples we are given power and authority to drive out all evil, heal sickness and addiction, and proclaim God's authority to all people? Do you view this power and authority as something we are given as individuals, or is there significance to the fact that we are called *together*?

Encounter the Exponential Aspect of the Miraculous in Scripture

Remind the group that early in the chapter, Mike Slaughter refers to the miracle of the feeding of the five thousand. Further on, he explores that miracle in more depth. Invite participants to quickly review the information in the chapter under the heading, "Exponential Increase." Ask the group to listen as a volunteer reads aloud Luke 9:10-17, paying attention to what roles Jesus and his disciples each play in the miracle.

After hearing the passage read, point out that this particular miracle story is so significant it is included in all four Gospels. Discuss some of the following:

- What would you imagine the disciples were thinking when Jesus said, "You give them something to eat"? Can you name a time when you felt a nudging from the Spirit to take on a calling, and yet it seemed overwhelming, if not impossible? How did you respond?
- The author observes that you and I, together in community, become the source for God's miracles. Do you think it makes a difference if we release our gifts together, rather than trying to take on a mission alone? Why or why not?

Ask someone to read aloud Deuteronomy 28:13, found in the chapter. Discuss:

- The author notes that Jesus' way of the cross turns our understanding of success, abundance, and leadership upside-down. How would you say this understanding of success differs from the message of the so-called prosperity gospel?
- Slaughter highlights the conditional nature of the command: If you pay attention to the commands of the Lord and carefully follow them, then you will experience the abundant life that Jesus promises. How would you define the abundant life?

Reflect on How We Might Respond

Call the group's attention to the posted reflection questions from the end of the chapter, discussed at the beginning of the session. Ask participants to name some of the opportunities for mission they are aware of in your church, neighborhood, or workplace.

Some of the opportunities may be initiatives that individual group members are already involved in, while others may be initiatives that one person or another is aware of and which the group could support or participate in.

With this information in mind, invite participants to take time to respond in writing in their journals to one or more of the questions. After allowing a few minutes for group members to reflect and write, ask one or two volunteers to report some of what they wrote. Encourage participants to continue to reflect on places where releasing their gifts could result in an exponential miracle.

WRAPPING UP

Closing Activity

Remind the group that the author describes an activity called "Name Change," where he invited the congregation to participate. He asked those in the congregation to write down what their "name" was before encountering Jesus. Later in worship, they were directed to mark out that name and to instead write down their new name in Christ.

Distribute index cards. Ask participants to use the cards to follow the author's instructions, then write some of their thoughts in doing so.

Closing Prayer

Offer a prayer, or ask a volunteer to offer a prayer, encouraging participants to envision Jesus as intercessor, sitting at the right hand of God. What would they ask Jesus as intercessor to help them do in their lives to participate in God's miracles?

2

MIRACLES COME WITH A COST

PLANNING THE SESSION

Session Goals

As a result of conversations and activities connected with this session, group members should begin to:

- explore the contrast between the values of the American Dream and those of the kingdom of God;
- explore insights about life priorities from Jesus' encounters on his final journey to Jerusalem;
- encounter a true sign of transformation on Zacchaeus's story; and
- reflect on how we might fast and feast as spiritual disciplines.

Scriptural Foundation

[Jesus] told them: "Take nothing for the journey—no staff, no bag, no bread, no money, no extra shirt."

(Luke 9:3)

Special Preparation

- Have materials available for anyone who did not bring a paper or electronic journal.
- For the activity on exploring contrasting values, head one large sheet of paper with "The American Dream" and another with "The Kingdom of God."
- For the activity of exploring Jesus' encounters, print the following on a large sheet of paper or a board. You will use this again in the reflecting activity.
  o Luke 9:57–58 (really understanding what we have signed up for);
  o Luke 9:59–60 (confronting excuses for our delayed obedience);
  o Luke 9:61–62 (rightly prioritizing our relationships).
- For the closing activity, choose a hymn of commitment, such as "Take My Life," and arrange for accompaniment. If you like, check online for a YouTube version of the hymn.

GETTING STARTED

Opening Activity

As participants arrive, welcome them. If there are any participants who were not present for session 1, offer a special welcome and make introductions. Ask a volunteer to briefly summarize what happened in that session.

Gather together. Ask the group to consider the following question:

- If you were asked to state the true message of Jesus in one or two sentences, what would you say?

Give participants a moment or two to jot down a response in their journals, then invite them to read their responses aloud. Tell the group that in this second session, they will explore more fully what it really means to make the decision to follow Jesus. They will examine the author's contention that such a decision clearly calls for a radical lifestyle adjustment, or as he expresses it, all in!

Opening Prayer

Pray together, using the following prayer or one of your own choosing:

Holy God, we come together again to encounter you in your living Word, trusting that where two or three of us are gathered together, there you will be, as you have promised. Guide us as we grapple with a radical understanding of what it means to truly follow your son, Jesus Christ. Open our minds to new understandings and our hearts to a new commitment to your call. Amen.

LEARNING TOGETHER

Video Study and Discussion

In session 2, we meet eighty-year-old Evelyn Alder, the manager of the Gleaning Place, and Mike Slaughter invites us to consider the implications of focusing on reordering our missional life priorities.

- What is the most striking thing to you about Evelyn Alder's achievements, in the light of her background and the challenges she has faced? Why?
- In interviewing Ms. Alder, Mike Slaughter asks her to name one of her favorite miracles she has observed in her work. What was her response?

- What are the words on the plaque displayed in the Gleaning Place, and how do you respond to the ideas it expresses? Are you in agreement with what it says about faith?

Book and Bible Study and Discussion

Explore Contrasting Values

Invite participants to reflect on the concept of the American Dream. Ask them to jot down in their journals the values they think are embodied in this concept. After allowing a few minutes for reflection and writing, ask participants to name values that come to mind. List these on the sheet headed "The American Dream."

Now invite them to reflect on and write down what values come to mind when they consider the kingdom of God. Record these ideas on the sheet headed "The Kingdom of God." Discuss some of the following together:

- Where, if at all, do you see contrasts in these lists of values?
- As you think honestly about your own life, which list most clearly reflects your priorities?
- In what ways might the common priorities that Slaughter names (getting a good education in order to have a prosperous career, raise a family, and so forth) distort our calling from God?
- Do you think it's possible to give these priorities a high ranking in one's life and still give allegiance to the values of the kingdom of God? Why or why not?

Invite a volunteer to read aloud this session's foundational Scripture (Luke 9:3) and ask the group to think about the following question:

- Why do you think Jesus asked his disciples to travel light?

23

Ask someone to read aloud Luke 12:13–21. Encourage the group to reflect in writing in their journals on one or more of the following:

- Has there been a time when you have been guilty of asking God to bless and prosper your own self-focused life plans? If so, what happened?
- What do you think it means to have the kingdom value of being rich toward God? How does that contrast with the cultural value of storing up possessions?
- Mike Slaughter observes that we are called by the Master to use our affluence for good in the lives of people who have neither influence nor affluence. He suggests that life is found in the intentional acts of giving our life gifts to others. How do you respond? What is life-giving for you? Why?

Explore Scriptural Insights about Life Priorities

The author asks us to imagine how different the world would look if Christians really followed Jesus rather than merely believing in Jesus. Form three groups to explore three encounters Jesus had on his final journey to Jerusalem, as posted by you before the session. Assign one of the posted passages to each small group.

Also suggest that each group review the information in the book that provides commentary on their passage. Ask them to discuss together their verses and what the author has to say about them, and then record on a large sheet of paper responses to the following:

- summarize major points gleaned from the passage or from the author's explanation;
- record comments about the passage; and
- raise questions about what participants have read—places where they may disagree or aspects of either the passage or the commentary that are unclear or confusing.

Allow several minutes for groups to explore their assigned verses, and then invite each small group to report on their discussion. After all three groups have reported, ask participants to consider the insights and main points the groups named, as well as the questions they surfaced. Then, if not already mentioned in their reports, discuss the following:

- How would you summarize the cost of following Jesus, as revealed in these verses?
- What does the story of the Dearings tell us about the cost of being part of a miracle? What rewards did you note?

Encounter a True Sign of Transformation

Ask someone to describe briefly what the author tells us about how tax collectors were viewed in the first century. Then invite a volunteer to read aloud the story of Jesus' encounter with Zacchaeus in Luke 19:1-10. Discuss some of the following:

- Next to Son of God, what title does the author say is the greatest title assigned to Jesus? Why?
- He suggests that God is able to achieve a miracle with the help of our own life mission when we are willing to be the friend of sinners. In our context, who would you identify as those groups comparable to tax collectors in Jesus' time? Which persons are despised because of their business practices or ethical behavior?
- Which of these persons or groups do you think would likely not be welcomed with open arms in our churches or in our homes? Why?
- The author observes that Zacchaeus, whose previous identity was centered in the status of position and wealth, now finds his identity in the priorities of Jesus' mission. What do you imagine was the cost to Zacchaeus of reordering his financial priorities?

Recall for the group the previous activity in which they contrasted the values of the American Dream with the kingdom of God values. Also briefly revisit last session's discussion on where one finds one's identity. Ask the group to reflect silently for a moment on the following:

- On what do I place my highest priorities? If it is on material possessions and financial security, to what degree, if at all, does this distract me from living out my identity as a follower of Jesus?

Reflect on Fasting and Feasting

Remind the group that during Lent and at other times of year, some Christians have taken on the practice of fasting, normally by abstaining from eating meat or some other food. The author tells us that the practice has been broadened today to include such practices as eliminating a habit, removing a distraction, or simplifying a lifestyle. But it may also mean feasting on a new life practice or strategy for reprioritizing one's life.

Invite participants to read over the suggestions offered by the author at the end of the chapter for possible ways God might be calling persons to fast during this study and beyond. Point out that in addition to the suggested ways to refrain from something, there are also ideas for ways to "feast" on a new practice or habit.

Revisit the previous activity where small groups explored three encounters Jesus had on his final journey to Jerusalem, calling attention again to the sheet posted for that activity. Ask participants to read over the author's suggestions for fasting (and feasting), and identify which suggestions might be ways of addressing the key idea in each of the three encounters. For example:

- Which suggestions might help a person explore that it really means to follow Jesus?

- Which suggestions might help one think about whether or not he or she is filling up time making excuses for not committing more fully to God's call?
- Which suggestions address the issue of prioritizing right relationships?

Also consider what insights emerged from exploring the story of Zacchaeus, and ask the group to check for suggestions that deal with transformation that might come from reordering one's financial priorities.

Ask participants to take time reading over what is suggested, and choose at least one of the suggested practices to pursue in the coming days. Or they may choose a practice that comes to mind that better fits their needs. Ask them to jot it in down in their journals and commit to that practice in the coming days.

WRAPPING UP

Ask someone to reread aloud this session's foundational Scripture, Luke 9:3. Then ask:

- Jesus commands us to leave behind the physical trappings of our lives as we embark on the Christian journey. But what spiritual resources will you need in order to do as the author suggests: to engage in a concentrated personal life assessment that might lead to reordering our missional life priorities?

Suggest that participants consider whether they need more concentrated and intentional Bible study or a more regular and focused time of prayer each day, as they move forward. They may also want to choose one or more partners in the group with whom to exchange e-mails or text messages to encourage them to keep up a regular time of devotion.

Invite those participants who wish to do so to respond, popcorn style, to the following:

- As I think about the cost of following Jesus, what I find disquieting or disturbing is . . .
- In exploring how I might partner in God's work in the world, I am excited by . . .
- I want to reflect further on . . .

Remind participants to read chapter 3 before the next session.

Closing Activity

Sing or recite the lyrics to "Take My Life" or another hymn of commitment.

Closing Prayer

Pray the following prayer:

God of miracles, we long to be a part of your redeeming work of justice in the world. But too often our excuses get in the way. We procrastinate, we dissemble, or we just get cold feet about the commitment such work may entail. By your spirit, guide us as we work to reorder our priorities to more clearly reflect a commitment to following Jesus, not just believing in him. Amen.

3

THE MIRACLE OF LOVE

PLANNING THE SESSION

Session Goals

As a result of conversations and activities connected with this session, group members should begin to:

- explore the nature of love and how we rightly order our love relationships;
- examine ways in which we picture God;
- encounter God's true identity in Jesus;
- encounter parables of God's redemptive love; and
- reflect on participating in the miracle of God's love.

Scriptural Foundation

"My command is this: Love each other as I have loved you. Greater love has no one than this: to lay down one's life for one's friends."

(John 15:12-13)

Special Preparation

- Provide writing materials for anyone who did not bring a notebook or an electronic device for journaling.
- For the activity exploring the nature of love, decide if you want to show a YouTube video of the Greek dance, perichoresis. Download and get the equipment for projecting the clip, or have participants view it on their smartphones.
- For the activity of examining images of God, print the following on a large sheet of paper or a board. You will also need five large sheets of paper and colored markers or crayons for each pair or group.
  - o wrathful god of vengeance;
  - o ancient white male;
  - o tribal god;
  - o god of the nation-state;
  - o cosmic traffic cop.
- For encountering the parable of the prodigal son, print on individual index cards the name of the three characters of the parable (younger son, older son, father). Prepare enough that each participant will have one, with one third of the cards for each character.
- For the reflecting activity, print the following on a large sheet of paper or a board:
  - o open up your home to neighbors with an open-table meal;

- o be part of or host a barrier-busting event within your community;
- o sign up for a mission experience or find a local mission opportunity; and
- o hold or join an ecumenical prayer meeting for your community.

GETTING STARTED

Opening Activity

As participants arrive, welcome them. Gather together. If group members paired up in the last session to encourage one another through texts or e-mails, ask them to touch base with their partners to discuss together how successful they were in trying out the practice of fasting or "feasting" to which they made a commitment. For those in the group who may have felt themselves less than successful, remind them that it takes time to form any habit. They may also have discovered the practice they chose was not a good fit, and they may want to try another practice.

Call participants' attention to the following open-ended prompt, inviting them to call out responses with whatever comes to mind,

- I love…

Encourage them to continue to offer as many responses as they can think of, from the names of cherished loved ones and friends to their favorite foods, sports teams, and so forth. When the group run out of responses, point out that love is defined in many ways, from attachment to the relatively trivial like a favorite dress or food to the strong and enduring emotions we may have for a spouse or a child. In this session, the group will explore the idea that love is the driving force behind every miracle.

Opening Prayer

Pray together, using the following prayer or one of your own choosing:

Steadfast God, we give thanks for your enduring presence and loving ways with us. Most of all, we are grateful for your gift of your son, who came to show us what you are like. Guide us as we encounter the transforming truth that in loving ourselves and others, we are most completely able to show our love for you. Amen.

LEARNING TOGETHER

Video Study and Discussion

In session 3 we meet Zach Williams, a police officer in Dayton, Ohio, who is working in his community to bring groups together. We explore the nature of love, grounded in relationship and finding its most comprehensive expression in Jesus Christ. Love, we discover, is the driving force behind every miracle.

- In previous sessions, participants have explored the role of community in realizing miracles. In response to a shooting in a Dayton Walmart, what was Zach's vision for addressing the anger and fear engendered by the incident? How did community come into play?
- How did Zach bring "God's party" to the neighborhood?

Book and Bible Study and Discussion

Explore the Nature of Love

Ask participants with smartphones to take the author's suggestion and search through their web browsers for scriptures about God's love. Invite volunteers to read aloud verses that resonate. Note that loving God, self, and others are inextricably woven together, and that rightly ordering our love relationships is key to participating in God's miracles.

Invite a volunteer to summarize briefly what the author wrote in his book about the Greek dance, perichoresis. If you like, show (or direct participants to view on their smartphones) a video clip of the dance on YouTube. Discuss:

- The author tells us that the mutual giving and receiving of perichoresis is the essence of how God the Father, Jesus Christ, and the Holy Spirit are in relationship. How do you respond to this description of the Trinity? Would you add anything to this understanding?

Have those with smartphones use Google for images of the Trinity. Ask:

- How does the analogy of perichoresis differ from other diagrams you have seen that seek to describe the Trinity?
- Mike Slaughter suggests that we are meant to be a part of this holy dance of relationship, with God and with one another. How, if at all, is this idea related to the commandment to love God and to love your neighbor as you love yourself?

Examine How We Picture God

Mike Slaughter observes that the way we picture God determines how we perceive ourselves and others. He notes that through the millennia, flawed theology has generated images of cultural deities that support some of the worst characteristics of human beings.

Call the group's attention to the posted list of images of God. Form five small groups or pairs, depending on the size of your group. Assign one of the posted images of God to each pair or group, and give each a large sheet of paper and colored markers or crayons. Ask them to read over the information about their assigned image in the chapter. Then ask them to create an illustration describing their image, using drawings, symbols, or just words and phrases.

Also ask them to discuss what the limitations are for viewing God in this particular way.

Back in the large group, ask each pair or group to explain its illustration and describe the limitations the participants discussed in conceiving of God in this way. Then discuss:

- Was there ever a time in your life when you would have perceived God as any one of these images describes God? If so, describe your understanding of God at that time. How and why did your view of God change?

Encounter God's True Identity in Jesus

The author tells us that in Jesus' life and teaching we have a living picture of who God is and what God values, and we see that God values human relationships over legalistic doctrines and people over ideologies. Discuss some of the following:

- The author contends that Bible idolatry is one of the heresies plaguing the church today. What does he mean by this? Do you agree or disagree?

Remind the group that in book chapter 2, the author asked us to imagine how different the world would look if Christians really followed Jesus rather than merely believing in Jesus. Form pairs. Ask one partner in each pair to read silently the parable of the good Samaritan (Luke 10:25-37) Ask the other to read the account of the woman at the well (John 4:1-30). After reading their assigned passage, ask each pair to discuss what the passage had to say about legalism versus relationship. In the large group, discuss the following:

- In these passages, which seems to take priority for Jesus— adhering to the religious rules and prohibitions of the time, or responding to the mandates of human relationships?

- Where do you see this same tension playing itself out in the church or in the culture today? Would you say that you come down on the side of adherence to the rules, or on the side of the priority of relating with love? Why?

Encounter Parables of God's Redemptive Love

The author reminds us of Jesus' unfailing love for lost, broken people. Randomly distribute the prepared index cards to participants, then ask a volunteer to read aloud Luke 15:11–32, the parable of the prodigal son. As the parable is read, ask them to listen from the perspective of the character printed on their card.

Following the reading, debrief by asking volunteers from each of the three perspectives to describe in character what they were thinking and feeling. Then discuss some of the following:

- The author observes that when false identity meets with our physical appetites, we are capable of doing the unthinkable. How do you respond?
- In describing how the father responded to his wayward son, the author notes that before we ever find our way even close to where we should be, God runs to us, has compassion for us, and throws loving arms around us. Have you ever experienced this sense of acceptance from God? What were the circumstances? How did you feel?
- Slaughter suggests that judgment creates distance in our relationship with both God and others—sometimes a physical distance, sometimes emotional or relational. What do you think?

Reflect on Participating in the Miracle of God's Love

The author poses the following question: How can you be a visible demonstration of the miracle of God's love? He offers some suggestions to begin thinking of how participants might respond. Invite the group to read over the suggestions you posted before the session (from the end of the book chapter). If there are mission initiatives in your local congregation or in your community that the group can identify, add those to the list.

Remind them that in session 1 of the study, they considered the following: Where are you sensing God at work right now in your church or community through divine intervention intersecting with human initiative? In that session they took some time to reflect in their journals on how they as individuals might release their gifts. Encourage them now to identify one idea from the list that appeals to them and form small groups to talk about how they might take action to demonstrate God's love. If there is an idea only one participant is interested in pursuing, encourage that person to talk to family members or friends about how they might act together on that idea.

WRAPPING UP

Closing Activity

In the author's discussion of the parable of the prodigal son, he speaks of the son's realization that he had strayed off the path he had intended his life to take, and his life plan wasn't working. Mike Slaughter suggests that we consider the following:

- Take time in your Christian journey to examine your own life path. Are you where you pictured you would be? Or better yet are you still on the life path that God has called you to be on?

Invite participants to draw a horizontal line on a page in their journals (or just make a list in an electronic journal) to create a life path in their journals and to note significant events or choices they have made. Encourage them to ponder where they are on their life journey, and where they might need to make a course correction.

Remind participants to read book chapter 4 before the next session.

Closing Prayer

Pray the following prayer or one of your own choosing:

Amazing God, we know you are the source of love. By your Spirit, guide us ever closer to aligning our gifts and skills with the path you intend us to take. And keep us ever more aware that in loving you, we are called to love our neighbors as ourselves. Amen.

4

ACTIVATE THE POWER OF FAITH

PLANNING THE SESSION

Session Goals

As a result of conversations and activities connected with this session, group members should begin to:

- explore the role of Scripture in Jesus' life;
- examine three key actions of faith;
- encounter faith in the midst of uncertainty; and
- reflect on activating faith.

Scriptural Foundation

Now on his way to Jerusalem, Jesus traveled along the border between Samaria and Galilee. As he was going into a village, ten men who had leprosy met him. They stood at a distance and called out in a loud voice, "Jesus, Master, have pity on us!"'

When he saw them, he said, "Go, show yourselves to the priest." And as they went, they were cleansed.

(Luke 17:11-14)

Special Preparation

- Have available writing materials for anyone who did not bring a journal.
- For the opening activity, print the following on a large sheet of paper or a board: Faith is the absence of doubt.
- Chapter 4 in the book presents the opportunity to explore several passages of Scripture. Depending on the amount of time available for the session, you may choose to focus on one passage for study rather than trying to do justice to all the passages, or you may confine your discussion to only a few selected questions.
- For reflecting on faith, print the following suggestions on a large sheet of paper or a board:
  - o pray about a struggle with unbelief;
  - o identify one proactive step to bring about a needed miracle; and
  - o evaluate the risk of taking next steps.
- Decide if you will sing the old hymn "Trust and Obey" as a closing activity. Obtain the lyrics and arrange for accompaniment. Both the text and accompaniment can be found online. Another option is to recite the lyrics together.
- For the closing prayer, print the Serenity Prayer on a board or a large sheet of paper. Or if you like, just refer participants to the prayer at the end of chapter 4.

GETTING STARTED

Opening Activity

As participants arrive, welcome them. If group members were part of a small group discussing possible mission opportunities in the last session, ask them to briefly touch base with others in their group about their progress.

Gather together. Call attention to the posted statement: Faith is the absence of doubt. Designate one side of your space as representing total agreement with the statement and the opposite side representing total disagreement. Ask participants to line up, finding a spot they think best represents where they would place themselves on a continuum from agreeing to disagreeing.

When everyone has found a place, ask volunteers to describe why they placed themselves where they did. Then summarize what Mike Slaughter says about Mark 9:14-24, noting that the words "I do believe; help me overcome my unbelief!" have become his personal prayer.

Tell the group that in this session they will explore what constitutes true faith and explore the tension between faith and doubt.

Opening Prayer

Pray together, using the following prayer or one of your own choosing:

Gracious God, we confess that we often struggle with our faith. We yearn to believe, but in the midst of our faith journey, sometimes doubts creep in. Make us aware of your presence with us today. Surround us with a sense of acceptance and create a safe space in which we can explore our doubts as well as our certainties. Amen.

LEARNING TOGETHER

Video Study and Discussion

In session 4, viewers are introduced to Chris Mills, a recovering drug addict and single parent of a young daughter. Mike Slaughter revisits the idea that faith and belief are not the same thing, and he discusses how faith can be activated.

- In response to the question of how faith has entered the picture, Chris Mills responds that if God could bring him through all the storms of his life, God can do anything. What storms has Mills endured? How would you feel if you had experienced those things, and what would you do?
- What does Mills mean when he says that he uses the mustard seed he has?
- In speaking of his daughter, Chris Mills observes that miracles produce miracles, and death produces death. What do you think he means? How do you respond?

Book and Bible Study and Discussion

Explore the Role of Scripture in Jesus' Life

The author contends that it is impossible to fully grasp the events surrounding the Easter event without embracing the full humanity of Jesus. Invite the group to quickly review the material under the heading, "A Fully Human Messiah." Ask them to cite evidence of Jesus' humanity as described by Mike Slaughter in this section. Then discuss some of the following:

- The author observes that God's love is so far beyond our human capacity that our love seems like hate in comparison. How do you respond? As you think about those you love the most, what does that suggest to you about the depth and breadth of God's love?

41

- Slaughter contends that faith is feeling fear in harrowing or difficult situations and trusting God's absolute love in spite of it. Can you name a time when you were desperately afraid and yet still trusted in God's love? Can you describe a time when fear overrode your discernment of that love? What happened?

Invite volunteers to read aloud the following passages: Psalm 31:5; Psalm 22:1; Psalm 91:11-12; Deuteronomy 8:3; Deuteronomy 6:13, 16. The author observes that Jesus not only studied Scripture; he lived by the Word of God. Invite group members to name passages of Scripture that provide them with comfort and strength in difficult times, and list these on a large sheet of paper or a board. If they are familiar with the substance of the passage but are not sure of the specific reference, encourage them to describe what the passage conveys and jot down a phrase or idea as a place marker.

If no one in the group can identify an exact reference, participants may be able to do a search on their smartphones. Encourage group members in the coming days to read and reflect on some of the passages their peers identified as meaningful.

Examine Three Key Actions of Faith

The author notes that miracles always have a deeper underlying purpose. This is why the miracles of Jesus are called "signs" in John's Gospel: they point to a deeper reality found in the person of Jesus. Invite a volunteer to read aloud Luke 17:11-19, the passage in which the foundational scripture for this session is found. Discuss:

- What was different about the healing experienced by the man who returned to thank Jesus?
- What does the author contend that this story tells us about how miracles are activated?

Ask the group to read aloud Matthew 14:22–33 in round-robin fashion, with each participant reading a verse in turn. Call the group's attention to the key actions of faith the author tells us are demonstrated by Peter in this passage.

Form small groups with three participants in each group. Ask one person in each group to consider the action of risking forward, one to consider failing forward, and one to look at praying forward. Ask them, as needed, to review the material in the chapter related to their assigned key action of faith. Allow the small groups a few minutes to review silently, then ask them to report what they read to the others in their small group of three.

In the large group, invite participants to report insights from their discussion, as well as questions that surfaced.

Encounter Faith in the Midst of Uncertainty

Mike Slaughter affirms that often we can't imagine risking forward because the storms in our lives are simply too overwhelming. Invite a volunteer to read aloud Luke 8:22–25. Discuss:

- The author observes that there is a difference in believing in God and believing God. What does he mean? Do you agree?
- Slaughter notes that when we allow fear to influence our decisions, it inhibits the miracles of God from being actualized in our lives. When, if ever, have you experienced this?
- He observes that sometimes we have invited Jesus into our boats, but we treat him like a life preserver and not like the captain. How do you interpret this? Do you agree?

In this chapter Slaughter names some "storms" in his life at the time he was writing. Invite participants to reflect on the following and then respond in writing in their journals:

- What current storms can you name that are troubling the waters—either personal storms or crises being faced by our nation or our world?

- What fears about these storms are preventing you from focusing on what is important? Where are you failing to risk forward? Where do you fear that you—or others who might influence the course of the storm—might fail? Are you praying forward? If not, how might you make your prayer life more effective and powerful?

Reflect on Activating Faith

Point out that at the end of the chapter, the author poses this question:

- How will you activate your faith in your journey with Jesus?

Call attention to the posted sheet with summaries of the suggestions Slaughter gives readers for some steps they might take. Encourage group members to choose one of these steps to focus on in the coming days or to commit to another step they might take that may have surfaced in their minds as they read and discussed the chapter. Tell the group that the author also suggested that participants consider praying the following prayer as a part of their devotional time: "I do believe; help me overcome my unbelief!"

WRAPPING UP

Ask the group to reflect on the following:

- How do I define a miracle?
- Where have I seen evidence of God's miraculous, transforming healing?
- In what ways, and to what degree, am I willing to take the risks involved in participating, through faith, in God's work of miracle making?

Remind participants to read chapter 5 before the next session.

Closing Activity

Tell participants that in a testimony meeting following a crusade led by Dwight L. Moody, a young man stood to speak. While it soon became clear he knew little Christian doctrine, he finished by saying, "I'm not quite sure—but I'm going to trust, and I'm going to obey." Someone present at the meeting, jotted down the words and gave them to John Sammis, who wrote the lyrics to the hymn "Trust and Obey." Tell the group that some of them may find the lyrics a simplistic approach to faith, belief, and action. Encourage them to think about what they might say about trusting God and about obedience if they were to write a new verse.

Sing or recite together the hymn "Trust and Obey."

Closing Prayer

Mike Slaughter observes that the favorite prayer of the Next Steps Recovery worshiping community, both at Ginghamsburg Church and beyond, has always been the Serenity Prayer attributed to Reinhold Niebuhr. Invite the group to pray this prayer together:

God grant me the serenity
To accept the things I cannot change;
Courage to change the things I can;
And wisdom to know the difference

Living one day at a time;
Enjoying one moment at a time;
Accepting hardships as the pathway to peace;
Taking, as He did, this sinful world
As it is, not as I would have it;
Trusting that He will make all things right
If I surrender to His Will;
So that I may be reasonably happy in this life
And supremely happy with Him
Forever in the next.

[Attributed to Reinhold Niebuhr, 1892–1971]

5

ACTIVATE THE POWER OF PRAYER

PLANNING THE SESSION

Session Goals

As a result of conversations and activities connected with this session, group members should begin to:

- explore four essential dynamics of prayer;
- examine day-to-day miracles;
- encounter how prayer precedes progress; and
- ponder transforming their prayer life.

Scriptural Foundation

One of those days Jesus went out to a mountainside to pray, and spent the night praying to God.

(Luke 6:12)

Special Preparation

- Have available writing materials for anyone who did not bring a journal.
- Decide which of the two alternatives you will utilize for exploring the four essential dynamics of prayer. If you choose to form pairs or small groups for discussion, you may nevertheless want to read through the suggested questions for option number 2 and choose one or two of the questions for discussion as you debrief.
- On a large sheet of paper or a board, print the following reflection ideas from the end of book chapter 5:
  o prioritizing prayer in advance of an important upcoming decision;
  o identifying low expectations and remembering God's promises;
  o revisiting God's past miracles to experience anew God's power and promise;
  o thanking God for day-to-day miracles; and
  o committing to waiting, obeying, expecting and/or acting to be part of what God wants to do through you.
- If desired for the wrap-up, get some small smooth florists' stones, available from a craft store or a florist shop.
- For the closing activity, get copies of the old hymn "Standing on the Promises" and arrange for accompaniment or reciting the lyrics. There are several versions of the hymn on YouTube.

GETTING STARTED

Opening Activity

As participants arrive, welcome them. Invite volunteers to report on what steps they took in the past week to activate their faith. Encourage each person to consider whether they were

47

successful in at least making a start. If someone confesses to feeling a failure on the step they chose to try, remind the group that it often takes time to form the habits that undergird a serious commitment. Suggest that they continue to make some effort to move forward.

Gather together. Ask participants to respond to the following question, posed to members of Ginghamsburg Church:

- Which spiritual discipline do you feel is the most important to your faith journey?
- Which discipline do you struggle the most to practice?

Point out that for the author, as for many in his congregation, the answer is the same for both questions: prayer. Tell the group that prayer was Jesus' most practiced discipline—the Gospels record more than sixty occasions when Jesus was in prayer. In this session, participants will explore the idea that the power of prayer demonstrated by Jesus is essential to the miracles that God will do in and through our own lives.

Opening Prayer

Pray together, using the following prayer or one of your own choosing:

O Holy God, like Jesus' disciples, we long for Jesus to teach us to pray. Yet we confess that knowing how to pray is not enough. Guide us as we seek to explore more deeply how and when and why we pray. By your spirit, nudge us not only into words, but into the silence of prayer, that we may hear your voice more clearly. Amen.

LEARNING TOGETHER

Video Study and Discussion

In session 5, we are introduced to Carolyn Slaughter, wife of the author. Together, the Slaughters discuss the central place prayer holds in their lives.

- Mike Slaughter says he finds it hard not to pray with faith and expectation when he is praying in a place where he has already witnessed God perform a miracle. What location is special to him? Is there a particular place that functions as holy ground for you? If so, where and why?
- For both the Slaughters, early morning is the time set aside for focused prayer. If you have been able to set aside a designated time for prayer, when is it? What is it about that time that works well for you?
- Mike and Carolyn Slaughter both confirm that resistance may be a recurring theme in answering God's call. What people can you identify who might help you deal with resistance?
- Fasting and journaling are among the prayer practices the couple names as important to them. What practices are significant in your prayer life?

Book and Bible Study and Discussion

Explore Four Essential Dynamics of Prayer

The author tells us that Jesus prayed at crucial moments in his ministry, including before his most remarkable miracles. He suggests that the same power of prayer is essential to the miracles that God will do in and through our lives.

Choose one of the following options for discussion:

Option Number 1:

Ask a volunteer to summarize briefly what the chapter tells us about the context of Joshua 3:1-8. Then invite someone else to read the passage aloud. Tell participants that in these verses they can experience the four dynamics of prayer at work: wait, obey, expect, and act.

Form four small groups or pairs. Assign one of the four dynamics to each group. Ask groups to read the information in the chapter on their assigned dynamic. If there are scriptural references with which participants are not familiar, ask them to look up and skim through the relevant passages. Then ask them to come up with two or three questions that can be posed to participants in the other three groups.

After allowing five or ten minutes for pairs or groups to work, ask each one to report briefly and to pose their questions to the large group for discussion. Also check option number 2 for any question that has not already surfaced in the conversation.

Option Number 2:

Invite the group to review what the author has to say about the context of Joshua 3:1–8, and then have a volunteer read the passage. Discuss some of the following:

- The author suggests that waiting in prayer is a time of listening, not of speaking. What is the downside of failing to allow the holy space for waiting?
- What is the meaning of the Hebrew name for God, *Yahweh*, and how does the author connect it to prayer?
- In preparing to cross the Jordan River into the Promised Land, Joshua directs the people to consecrate themselves. How does the author define consecration?
- What does the author mean when he says that praying in Jesus' name is a whole lot bigger than merely saying his name ("in the name of Jesus")? How do you feel about this?
- In your opinion, what does it mean that expectation determines outcome? Has this been your experience? What were the circumstances?
- Mike Slaughter comments that his life experience has proven to him that where God gives vision, he also gives provision. What does he mean?
- What does the author mean by the statement that it is only when the Jordan Rivers in our lives are at flood stage that God's supernatural miracle is both possible and evident?

Examine Day-to Day Miracles

Mike Slaughter calls our attention to the role that gratitude plays in realizing and recognizing miracles in our daily lives. Ask participants to review the specific scriptural examples he gives when gratitude preceded a miracle. Discuss the following:

- Faith means trusting God even when the answer appears to be no. Can you name a time when the answer to your prayers seemed to be no? What were the circumstances? How did you react, and what was the impact, if any, on your faith?

Invite participants to name aloud some examples of what they would identify as God's everyday miracles. Discuss:

- The author suggests that seeing God in the everyday makes it easier to trust God when facing a crisis. When, if ever, has this been your experience?

Encounter How Prayer Precedes Progress

The author reminds us that God is not only inviting us to experience the dynamics of prayer, but also to be part of what he calls God's "kingdom of God" mission to all of planet earth. He notes that God plans to accomplish this miraculous restoration through us.

Nehemiah's story provides an example of how prayer precedes progress when it comes to miracles of restoration. Invite the group to review what the author has to say in setting the context for considering Nehemiah's prayer. Then ask a volunteer to read aloud Nehemiah's prayer in chapter 1:4–11. Discuss:

- What actions did Nehemiah take before praying? What function did each action serve?

Ask participants to read over Nehemiah's prayer silently and refer to the author's commentary. Then ask them to record in their journals each step the author suggests we can find in the prayer. After allowing time for participants to reflect and write, ask them to partner up with someone close by and discuss the steps they recorded.

Remind participants that prayer is a prelude to action and that everyday miracles and monumental miracles are possible when we activate the power of prayer in our lives. Ask them to reflect on the following question with which the author challenges us:

- Where is God inviting you to be part of God's restorative purpose, God's coworker in bringing about extraordinary miracles that redeem the lost and set the oppressed free?

Ponder Transforming Prayer Life
Mike Slaughter poses the following question:

- How will you transform your prayer life in your journey with Jesus?

In response to that question, call the group's attention to the posted suggestions that Slaughter gives at the end of the chapter. Ask participants to read over those suggestions and jot down in their journals one or more they will explore in the coming week.

Take a few moments for participants to offer other ideas for transforming their prayer life that may have surfaced during the session. Encourage them to also note in their journals any of these ideas that appeal to them.

WRAPPING UP

Remind the group that after the Hebrew people had safely crossed the flooded Jordan River into the Promised Land, God's first directive was to erect a memorial made of stones from the river to serve as a reminder of God's miracle for future days when other significant obstacles would need to be overcome.

If you were able to obtain stones before the session, distribute one to each participant and ask them to reflect in silence on times when they have experienced God's miraculous power in their lives or when God's promises seemed very sure. After a few moments of silence, ask each person to bring their stone forward and place it on the table, describing that event in a few words or simply placing it there in silence. Encourage those who would like to do so to take home a stone as a tangible reminder.

Remind participants to read book chapter 6 before the final session.

Closing Activity

In his discussion of praying with great expectation, Mike Slaughter cites the example of Daniel, who ignored the royal decree to pray only to the king of the land and continued his discipline of praying to God three times daily. Slaughter observes that this story brings to mind the old Sunday school hymn "Standing on the Promises." Sing or recite the hymn together.

Closing Prayer

Mike Slaughter tells us that John Wesley's covenant prayer still gives him chills each time he reads it. Invite the group to join you in this adapted version of the prayer:

I am no longer my own, but yours.
Put me to what thou will, rank me with whom you will....
I freely and heartily yield all things to your pleasure and disposal.
And now, O glorious and blessed God, Father, Son and Holy Spirit,
You are mine, and I am yours.
So be it.... Amen

(*Methodist Worship Book*, p. 29)

6

ACTIVATE HEALTH AND HEALING

PLANNING THE SESSION

Session Goals

As a result of conversations and activities connected with this session, group members should begin to:

- explore some healing miracles of Jesus;
- examine three components in the partnership of healing;
- consider responding together with compassion; and
- ponder activating individual miracles of health and healing.

Scriptural Foundation

At sunset, the people brought to Jesus all who had various kinds of sickness, and laying his hands on each one, he healed them.

(Luke 4:40)

Special Preparation

- Have available writing materials for anyone who did not bring a journal.
- On a large sheet of paper or a board, print the following health statistics:
  - o According to the Center for Disease Control (CDC), heart disease, the nation's number one killer, claims over six hundred thousand US lives annually; and
  - o In the United States, two in three adults are considered to be overweight or obese; ninety-one people in the United States die every day from opioid overdose.
- For pondering how to activate miracles of healing, print the following on a large sheet of paper or a board:
  - o Find a group for accountability for life change;
  - o begin to exercise;
  - o check for treatments and faith-based supports for substance abuse; and
  - o commit to a new spiritual, emotional, mental, or physical practice.
- If you decide to use anointing as the closing activity, get some oil, a small bowl, and a cloth. Or you may prefer to use the hymn "Called as Partners in Christ's Service." Words and music can be found online.

GETTING STARTED

Opening Activity

As participants arrive, welcome them to this final session in the study. Gather together. Invite them to partner with someone sitting nearby and spend a few minutes discussing which suggestion from the previous session they explored in order to begin to transform their prayer life. Or perhaps the ideas suggested by the author sparked another idea that they tried.

After a few minutes, invite one or more volunteers to describe briefly what they tried and how it worked. As in the past session, emphasize that forming new habits takes time, and encourage group members to continue practicing prayer.

Call attention to the posted statistics about health. Invite participants with smartphones to do a search for other statistics, and add them to the list. Then ask the group to consider in silence the following questions:

- Generally, how healthy are you? What are the greatest challenges to your health and well-being?
- In your opinion, which issues related to health and well-being present the greatest challenges for our nation? for the world?

Remind the group that restoring people to physical, mental, and spiritual health was a key component of Jesus' earthly ministry. In this final session they will explore the idea that we are to be active participants in our own healing and in the healing of the world.

Opening Prayer

Pray together, using the following prayer or one of your own choosing:

Loving God, we acknowledge that you want all of creation to experience that sense of wholeness and well-being that we call shalom. Yet we know that for most of the world's people, shalom seems out of reach. We ourselves often confuse material success and the relentless acquisition of stuff with the abundant life that is ours in Christ. Guide us as we explore what it means to claim abundant life for ourselves. Confront us with what we are called to do and be, as your partners in securing health and well-being for all. Amen.

LEARNING TOGETHER

Video Study and Discussion

In session 6, we meet Chastity Slone, Mike Slaughter's personal trainer for the past seventeen years. With her help, Slaughter encourages us to overcome any obstacle that opposes God's purpose for our lives as we seek to live out our days in health and wholeness.

- The author confesses that at the time he had a serious health incident, he was ignoring his own personal health. In terms of partnering with God on God's miraculous acts in the world, why it is important to take one's own health seriously?
- What is the importance of consistency in training one's body? How, if at all, is physical fitness important in maintaining spiritual health?
- Slaughter observes that discipline is doing the unnatural. How do you respond? Would you agree that all discipline is sacrificial?

Book and Bible Study and Discussion

Explore a Healing Miracle of Jesus

Invite a volunteer to read aloud John 5:1–9a. Then ask participants to review the material in the chapter under the heading "Do You Want to Get Well?" Ask one or two persons to describe the function of the Pool of Bethesda.

Before beginning a discussion of this passage, emphasize for the group that many of us come from a place of privilege because of our race, class, gender, or ability. Questions about our sense of powerlessness and its sometimes paralyzing effects should not be confused with the very real marginalization many people experience because of life situations truly beyond their control. With this in mind, discuss some of the following:

- We read that in the first century, physical dysfunction was code for spiritual illness. In our time, what is problematic about this way of thinking? Do you think there is ever a connection between physical ailments and spiritual wellness? Why or why not?
- Naming our places of suffering or brokenness, says the author, is always the first step toward transformation. Do you agree? Why or why not?
- How does Mike Slaughter define spiritual impotency? What is the potential trap involved in considering ourselves as victims, as powerless?
- Have you ever made paralyzing excuses for your own inaction? What were the circumstances?
- The author observes that we can learn to become comfortable in our current state of unhealth. When, if at all, have you experienced this?
- The author refers to the Trinity. What does he mean when he says that we too are triune beings? If we acknowledge that this is true, what are the implications? What do you think this concept tells us about the abundant life?

Examine Components in the Partnership of Healing

The story about the Pool of Bethesda lifts up three components of the part we are to play in bringing about miracles of healing: get

58

up, pick up, and walk. Invite participants to take a closer look at these components.

With the story in mind, ask participants to form three small groups or pairs. Assign one of the three components of healing to each group or pair. Ask participants to reread the Scripture passage and discuss it as it relates to their assigned component, with each person jotting down notes about insights, questions, and areas where they may be discerning that God is calling them to act.

After a few minutes, ask participants to change up the small groups, forming groups of three composed of one person from each of the three previous groups. (If you have a small number of participants, you may want to discuss in the large group.) Ask participants now to report to this new group on their discussion about their assigned component.

In the large group, discuss the following:

- What implications of the three components do I see for my own personal health and well-being?
- Based on the scripture and the discussion, what can we conclude about our role in working toward God's intention of health and well-being for the whole world?

Consider Responding Together with Compassion

The author tells us that we and our churches are also called to be empowering centers for healing and renewal in our communities and beyond. Invite participants to review the passages Mike Slaughter lists, where Jesus showed compassion for the throngs of people seeking his help and healing power. Ask:

- How do you define compassion? Is it merely an emotional response to a person or situation in need of healing, or it is something more?

Ask participants to reflect on how in the previous activity they explored the meanings of get up, pick up, and walk. Then ask participants to call out, popcorn style, situations in which they think God might be calling them as individuals or as a faith community to get up, pick up, and walk on behalf of the world God loves. Jot down these situations as they are named.

With a show of hands, ask the group to identify two situations or issues to consider in more depth. Then have them self-select from the issues and form two working groups. Ask them to discuss the following:

- How might you and your faith community respond by being agents of compassion creating healing and hope?

After allowing time for groups to work, ask each group to report the ideas they generated for both individual and communal responses of compassion. Encourage them to reflect further on how they might act as individuals. Also have them consider joining some congregational initiative already in place or to think about starting a new initiative of compassionate service.

Ponder Activating Miracles

The author poses the following question:

- What is the most important new spiritual, emotional, mental, or physical practice for which you need to get up, pick up, and walk to achieve health?

Call the group's attention to the posted list of possible steps to take in order to activate miracles of health and healing in their own lives. Encourage them to reflect on the suggestions and to consider making a commitment to work long-term on establishing new, more healthy habits in their lives or on breaking habits that have led to destructive patterns in their lives.

Participants may want to record the commitments in their journals, maintaining their privacy about personal choices. But suggest that participants may want to join in a partnership of prayer, committing to praying daily for one another. Encourage them to seek out a prayer partner in the group, or some other person they know. You might also suggest that group members take turns sending a weekly e-mail or text to the rest of the group reminding them to pray for one another.

WRAPPING UP

Throughout this study, participants have explored the idea that when God acts, God always acts through people. Both Old and New Testament scriptures reveal that miracles typically have two dimensions: divine intervention and human responsibility.

Note that the book introduction posed the following question:

- Where is God calling you to heal, teach, preach, redeem, and restore that which is broken, struggling, or suffering in the world God loves?

As they reflect on this question, invite participants to respond to the following open-ended statements as they feel called to do so:

- As I consider my true identity and purpose in Christ, I will...
- As I reflect on the fact that miracles come with a cost, I will...
- As I ponder how I might participate in the miracle of God's love, I will...
- As I consider activating my faith I will...
- As I think about transforming my prayer life, I will...
- As I consider how to partner with God in acts of healing and wholeness, I will...

Ask participants to review in their journals the various practices and steps they have committed to trying. Acknowledge that in all likelihood, few participants will continue all the suggested steps and practices on a long-term basis. But encourage them to commit to continuing at least one.

Closing Activity

Tell the group that the practice of anointing with oil has a long history. Throughout the Old Testament, the anointing of a person acknowledged God's choosing that person as set apart for a special vocation or call. Anointing was also a practice associated with restoring a person to health and wholeness.

Invite participants to form a circle, and tell the group that they have the opportunity to be anointed. Say that people who choose to opt out of the activity should simply indicate the desire to pass by shaking their head.

For those who choose to participate, they will each in turn reach for the bowl, then turn to the person on their right, dip a thumb into the oil, and make the sign of the cross on the person's forehead, saying, "[Name], as you are anointed with oil, may you be anointed with the Holy Spirit." Then that person should turn to the person on their right and do the same. Have participants continue around the circle until all are anointed who wish to be.

Closing Prayer

Pray the following prayer or one of your choosing:

Gracious God, we are in awe of your loving, redeeming power! By your Spirit, equip us to be your partners in healing a hurting world. Sharpen our awareness of the world's wounds, and grant us the courage, the will, and the commitment to make ourselves available to your purposes. Amen.

.

Made in the USA
Lexington, KY
09 February 2019